1 Trace and write the joins.

pp ____________ *bb* ____________

AF080427

2 Add suffixes to the root words.

Root word	Adding suffix: *-ing*	Adding suffix: *-ed*	Adding suffix: *-er*
zip			
skip			
rob			
grab			
appoint			
gobble			

3 Write a sentence using a *pp* word and a *bb* word.

Check:
- your ascenders and descenders are parallel
- your spelling of each word with its suffixes.

Find two words to tick and two to improve. Rewrite them.

1 Trace and write the break letters.

x ______________________ z ______________________

2 Add the word beginnings to the word endings and write the words you make.

periment  hale

______________ ______________

ex

treme perience

______________ ______________

3 Write the words you made and sort them into the table. Note that some of the words can be both nouns and verbs.

Nouns	Verbs	Adjectives
experiment		

4 Write a word with *z* at the beginning, a word with *z* in the middle, a word which ends in *z* and a word with *zz*.

____

____

____

____

Check:

- your breaks to and from *x* and *z*
- your spelling of the words with prefix *ex*-.

Find two examples of break letters to tick and two to improve.
Rewrite them.

CAMBRIDGE

PENPALS for Handwriting

Workbook

4

Name .... Class ....

1 Trace and write the joins.

ph ____________ pl ____________ bl ____________

2 Trace and write the words.

the playful dolphin ____________________________

3 Make and write noun phrases using one word from each of these sets.

the	black	photograph
	blue	phone
	purple	planet
a	sensible	blind
	plain	people

____

____

____

____

____

4 Write your own noun phrase using words with *ph*, *pl* or *bl*.

____

____

Check:
- your joins from *b* and *p* are correct
- your noun phrases make sense.

Find two joins to tick and two to improve.
Rewrite them.

1 Trace and write the joins.

pu ______ pi ______ pe ______

bu ______ bi ______ be ______

2 Add the prefix to each of the endings. Write the words you make.

bio: sphere ______ logy ______ graphy ______

bi: nocular ______ ceps ______ cycle ______

3 Write two sentences using some of the words you made.

Check:

- your joins from *p* and *b*, no ascender
- your spelling of your words with prefixes.

Find two examples to tick and two to improve. Rewrite them.

1 Trace and write the joins.

pa ______ po ______ ps ______

ba ______ bo ______ bs ______

2 Trace and write the words.

possibly ______ boldly ______ perhaps ______

probably ______ on balance ______

3 Complete the sentences using the adverbials above.

1. ______, I'll meet you later.
2. ______, we shall march up the hill.
3. ______, I will wait for you after all.
4. ______, I'd prefer to go on my own.

4 Write a sentence using the word *possibly*.

______

______

Check:
- your joins from *p* and *b* to anticlockwise letters
- your sentences make sense
- your spelling of the adverbials.

Find two words to tick and two to improve.
Rewrite them.

1 Trace and write the sentence.

"Why did the chicken cross the road?"

Rex

What do you get if you cross a kangaroo with a skyscraper?

Zoe

A high jumper!

2 Write the joke as direct speech.

Rex said

3 Write how many of each punctuation mark you used.

“	”	?
!	.	,

Check:

- your letter spacing in words
- your punctuation.

Find two examples of good spacing to tick and two to improve.
Rewrite them.

1 Trace and write the joins.

in ________ im ________ il ________ ir ________

2 Trace the words. Add a prefix from above. Write the new words you make.

Root word	With a prefix
active	________
perfect	________
mature	________
responsible	________
legal	________

3 What happens to the meaning of the root word when you add the prefix?

____

Check:

- your letter sizing
- your spelling of the words with prefixes.

Find two examples of equal letter sizing to tick and two to improve.
Rewrite them.

____

____

1 Trace and write the sentence.

Zane was reading his friends' books.

2 Trace and write the sentences. Add the capital letters and punctuation.

1. the boys forgot the girls books

2. the girls were excited about the babies toys

3. the childrens favourite game was Z-Box

3 Now add the apostrophes to show ownership of the books, toys and game.

Check:

- the size of your capitals compared to the size of your lower case letters
- your punctuation marks.

Find two words to tick and two to improve. Rewrite them.

1 Finish the chart. Write quickly. Time yourself.

Personal pronouns	I	you	he	she	it	we	you	they
Personal pronouns	me	____	____	____	____	us	____	them
Possessive pronouns	mine	____	____	hers	____	____	____	____

2 Write a sentence using all three types of pronoun.

____

____

Check:
- the chart. Swap with a partner. Is it correct?
- the smoothness of your handwriting.

Find two words to tick for fluency and two to improve.
Rewrite them.

____

____

1 Trace and write the word. Write another word with *ph* in it.

dolphin ____________________ ☐

2 Trace the words. Write another word with *bl* and one with *bi*.

blue ____________ *bicycle* ____________ ☐☐

3 Trace the words. Write another word with *bb* and one with *pp*.

robber ____________ *zipper* ____________ ☐☐

4 Join these words using the joins you know.

exercise ____________ amazing ____________ ☐☐

5 Trace the words. Write another word with *im* and one with *il*.

imagine ____________ *illegible* ____________ ☐☐

6 Rewrite and punctuate the speech in the sentence.

hello this is important
please can you listen ☐

Mark and score. /10

1 Trace and write the joins.

ll ______ dd ______ th ______ lk ______

bb ______ tt ______

2 Trace and write the words.

descended ______ disciplined ______

scientist ______ ascended ______

3 Choose a word from above to fill the gaps. Rewrite each sentence.

1. The ______ worked in a very ______ way.

______

2. He ______ the laboratory stairs, looked at the stars and then ______ again.

______

______

Check:

- your ascenders. Are they parallel?
- your spelling of the words.

Find two words with parallel ascenders to tick and two to improve.
Rewrite them.

______

______

1 Trace and write the joins.

tion ______ tion ______

2 Make nouns by adding *-tion* **to each of these verbs.**

1. observe + tion = ______
2. classify + tion = ______
3. imagine + tion = ______
4. prepare + tion = ______
5. inform + tion = ______

3 Write the spelling rule for adding the suffix *-tion***.**

Words ending in *t*: ______

Words ending in *e*: ______

Words ending in *d*: ______

Check:
- your break letters
- your ascenders are parallel
- the spelling of your *-tion* nouns.

Find two words with parallel ascenders to tick and two to improve.
Rewrite them.

______

______

1 Trace and write between the lines.

brake break

meet meat

peace piece

great grate

2 Write a homophone for each word. Write between the lines.

mane meddle

scene bawl

Check:

- the size of your letters
- the spelling of the homophones.

Find two words with good letter sizing to tick and two to improve.

Rewrite them.

1 Trace and write the joins.

ture ______ ture ______

2 Trace and write the words.

adventure ______ captured ______

signature ______ picture ______ creature ______

3 Rewrite each sentence. Check that the height, length and width of similar letters is equal.

It was an ______ storybook.

______

The princess ______ the ______.

______

She scribbled her ______ on the ______.

______

Check:

- the proportion of your letters
- the spelling of the *-ture* words.

Find two words with good letter proportion to tick and two to improve.

Rewrite them.

______

______

1 Trace and copy the joins.

ssion ______ ssion ______

2 Make noun phrases using one word from each of these sets.

Determiner	Adjective	Noun
the	interesting	discussion
an	colourful	admission
a	surprising	expression
	curious	procession

3 Write your own noun phrase using a -ssion word. Watch your spacing.

Check:
- the spacing between the letters
- the spelling of the -ssion words
- the noun phrases make sense.

Find two words with good letter spacing to tick and two to improve.
Rewrite them.

1 Trace and write the sentence. Underline all of the words with an *ay* sound.

They are our neighbours from number eighty.

2 Choose the correct spelling for the *ay* sound. Rewrite each word.

*w*______ *ob*______

*sl*______ *tr*______

______*teen*

3 Write a sentence to include at least two of these spellings.

Check:

- the spacing between the words
- your spelling of the words with the *ay* sound.

Find two words with *ay* joins to tick and two to improve.

Rewrite them.

1 Trace the words carefully, then write them at speed.

roared ______ yelled ______

muttered ______ whispered ______

2 Choose a word from above to fill the gaps. Then add punctuation.

1. Get out of my way ______ the giant

2. I can help you to get down ______ the rescuer

3. I'm not sure what to do are you ______ my partner

4. I'm too sleepy now ______ the child

3 Write how many of each punctuation mark you used.

“		”		?	
!		.		,	

Check:
- your punctuation
- your writing is easy to read even when you write at speed
- your punctuation marks.

Find two words to tick and two to improve.
Rewrite them.

1 Trace and write the words.

I was ______ he/she/it was ______

you were ______ we were ______

they were ______

2 Write the sentences below, correcting the mistakes. Write neatly and carefully.

1. We was excited about the cinema.

______

2. I were going to get an ice-cream.

______

3. They was excited too. ______

4. When we met up we was happy.

______

Check:
- your grammar. Did you correct all the mistakes in the verb *to be*?
- the smoothness of your handwriting.

Find two examples of fluency to check and two to improve. Rewrite them.

______

______

1 Trace and write the words.

mine ______ yours ______ hers ______ his ______

its ______ ours ______ yours ______ theirs ______

2 Write a pronoun from above in each of the gaps. Rewrite the sentences neatly at speed.

1. I like this bag; it's ______

______

2. She has a new phone; it's ______.

______

3. The dog is happy to see us; he's wagging ______ tail.

______

4. They let us ride in their sports car; it's ______.

______

3 Check your grammar. Write a sentence using a pronoun you did not use above.

______

______

______

Check:
- the smoothness of your handwriting at speed
- your use of pronouns.

Find two words to tick and two to improve. Rewrite them.

______

______

1 Trace the word. Write another word with *sci* in it.

scientist ____________________ ☐

2 Trace the word. Write another word ending in *-tion*.

invention ____________________ ☐

3 Trace the sentence. Punctuate the speech in the sentence. Add your name.

I can punctuate speech correctly declared ☐

____________________. ☐ ☐

4 Trace the sentence. Fill the gaps with the correct verb form of the verb *to be*.

We __________ learning about the ☐

verb 'to be' and I __________ pleased. ☐

5 Trace the sentence. Add a possessive pronoun.

This is my handwriting check; ☐

it's ____________________.

Mark and score. / 8

1 Trace and write the joins.

ou ou

2 Trace and copy the phrase. Keep x-height letters between the lines.

trouble in the countryside.

3 Trace and write the words.

country

loud

double

about

found

touch

4 Sort the words into words with *ou* that sound like:

young	proud

Check:
- the size of your letters is similar
- your spelling of the *ou* words.

Find two words to tick and two to improve.
Rewrite them.

1 Trace and write. Use the lines to help with checking your letter proportions.

The pyramids in Egypt.

3 Trace and write the words.

crystal

gym

python

mystery

beyond

rhyme

4 Sort the words into words with *y* that sound like:

myth	*sty* **or** *yak*

Check:
- the proportions of your letters
- your spelling of *y* words.

Find two words to tick and two to improve.
Rewrite them.

1 Trace and write the joins.

ous ______ ous ______

2 Trace and write the phrase. Check your letter and word spacing.

The enormous rhinoceros.

3 Make and write noun phrases using one word from each of these sets.

Determiner	Adjective	Noun	Prepositional phrase
a	serious	hippopotamus	in a muddy swamp
an	jealous	monster	in a towering rage
this	enormous	sister	under the magic mountain

1. ______
2. ______
3. ______

Check:
- the spacing between letters and words
- your spelling of -ous words
- your noun phrases make sense.

Find two examples of good spacing and two to improve.

1 Trace and write the sentence.

The next day, Harry woke up with a start.

2 Rewrite each sentence with a fronted adverbial. Check the size, proportion and spacing of your writing.

1. Jarvia went to see Harry later that day.
2. Harry felt better the next morning.
3. They both went out after lunch.
4. They met friends in the park in the evening.

Check:

- the size, proportion and spacing of your writing
- your use of fronted adverbials
- you added a comma after each fronted adverbial.

Find two examples of good size, proportion and spacing to tick and two to improve.
Rewrite them.

1 Trace and write the phrases.

I have done

he/she/it has done

you have done

we have done

they have done

you have done

Check:
- the smoothness of your handwriting
- your corrections to the verb *to do*.

Find two examples of smooth writing to tick and two to improve.
Rewrite them.

2 Write the sentences, correcting the mistakes. Write neatly but at speed.

1. I done it really well.
2. We done it already.
3. They done it with us.
4. You done it better than I done it.

1 Trace and write the words.

dis ______ dis ______

2 Write each word twice without stopping. Tick the one that is most fluent.

misunderstanding disappointment

3 Add *mis-* or *dis-* to make new words.

______ + agree = ______
______ + behave = ______
______ + trust = ______
______ + like = ______
______ + lead = ______
______ + appear = ______

4 What happens when you add *mis-* to *spell*?

______

Check:
- the smoothness of your handwriting at speed
- your spelling of words with *dis-* and *mis-* prefixes.

Find two examples of fluency to tick and two to improve.
Rewrite them.

1 Write the pronouns.

I me mine ____________ you yours ____________

she her hers ____________ he him his ____________

we us ours ____________

they them theirs ____________

2 Choose the right pronoun from above to fill the gaps.

I — Give it to ____________.
It's ____________!

He — I'll give it to ____________.
It's ____________!

We — Give it to ____________.
It's ____________!

They — I'll give it to ____________.
It's ____________!

Check:
- your break letters are not joined
- your use of pronouns.

Find two examples of break letters to tick and two to improve.
Rewrite them.

____

____

1 Fill in the gaps to complete the alphabet.

a b _ d _ _ g h i _ _ l m

_ _ _ _ r _ t _ v _ _ _ _

2 Now write the complete print alphabet with no exit flicks on your letters. So a not *a*, d not *d*.

a b c d

3 Write your name and address using print.

4 What do we use print letters for? Why?

Check:

- your print alphabet letters. There should be no exit flicks
- the presentation of your print letters.

Find two examples of print letters to tick as well-formed letters and two to improve. Rewrite them.

1 Finish each word. Write it in full. These are all joins you will find in your book.

1. ele____nt
2. ___anket
3. ___cycle
4. ___dal
5. pro____ly
6. ___ssibly
7. ro___er
8. zi___er
9. e___periment
10. ama___ed
11. ___portant
12. ___legal
13. l___ratory
14. imagina____
15. an enorm____ pyramid
16. adven____
17. discu____
18. We ____ (to be)
19. I me____
20. They ____ theirs

po pe im x abo bab them
ssion were mine tion ph
pp bb z bl bi il ture ous

Remember to think about size, spacing, proportion, speed and fluency. Give yourself a score out of 5 for each.

1 Fill the gaps to complete the alphabet.

A ___ C ___ ___ F ___ ___ ___ J K ___ ___

___ O ___ ___ ___ S T ___ V ___ X ___ Z

2 Write these words in capitals.

danger ______________ no entry ______________

stay out ______________ poison ______________

no entry ______________ one way ______________

Check:

- your capitals.

Find two examples to tick as correctly-formed capital letters, and two to improve.
Rewrite them.

____

____

Certificate

for completing

PENPALS *for* Handwriting 4

awarded to

NAME ______________________________

DATE ______________ SIGNED ______________

University Printing House, Cambridge CB2 8BS, United Kingdom

One Liberty Plaza, 20th Floor, New York, NY 10006, USA

477 Williamstown Road, Port Melbourne, VIC 3207, Australia

314–321, 3rd Floor, Plot 3, Splendor Forum, Jasola District Centre, New Delhi – 110025, India

103 Penang Road, #05-06/07, Visioncrest Commercial, Singapore 238467

Cambridge University Press is part of the University of Cambridge.

It furthers the University's mission by disseminating knowledge in the pursuit of education, learning and research at the highest international levels of excellence.

Information on this title: www.cambridge.org

First published 2015

20 19 18 17 16 15 14 13 12

Printed in Poland by Opolgraf

A catalogue record for this publication is available from the British Library

ISBN 978-1-84565-385-9

Acknowledgements

www.cambridge.org

Illustrations by Matthew Britton
Cover design and layout by me&him
Authors: Gill Budgell and Kate Ruttle

CAMBRIDGE UNIVERSITY PRESS
www.cambridge.org

CAMBRIDGE

PENPALS for Handwriting

4

Workbook

Name .... Class ....

Relative size of capitals

1 Trace and write the sentence.

Zane was reading his friends' books.

2 Trace and write the sentences. Add the capital letters and punctuation.

1. the boys forgot the girls books

2. the girls were excited about the babies toys

3. the childrens favourite game was Z-Box

3 Now add the apostrophes to show ownership of the books, toys and game.

Check:

- the size of your capitals compared to the size of your lower case letters
- your punctuation marks.

Find two words to tick and two to improve.
Rewrite them.

CAMBRIDGE

PENPALS *for* Handwriting

Workbook

4

Name .... Class ....

CAMBRIDGE

PENPALS for Handwriting

4

Workbook

Name

Class

CAMBRIDGE

PENPALS for Handwriting

Workbook

4

Name

Class

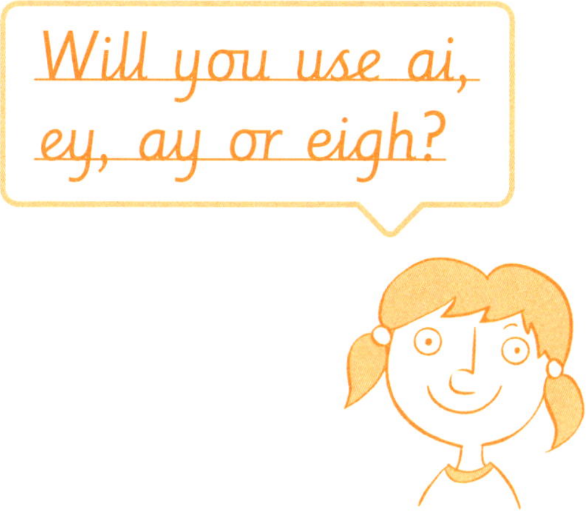

CAMBRIDGE

PENPALS *for* Handwriting

4

Workbook

Name

Class

CAMBRIDGE

PENPALS *for* *Handwriting*

Pack of 10

Year 4 / Primary 5 Workbook

CAMBRIDGE
UNIVERSITY PRESS

University Printing House, Cambridge CB2 8BS, United Kingdom

One Liberty Plaza, 20th Floor, New York, NY 10006, USA

477 Williamstown Road, Port Melbourne, VIC 3207, Australia

314–321, 3rd Floor, Plot 3, Splendor Forum, Jasola District Centre, New Delhi – 110025, India

103 Penang Road, #05-06/07, Visioncrest Commercial, Singapore 238467

Cambridge University Press is part of the University of Cambridge.

It furthers the University's mission by disseminating knowledge in the pursuit of education, learning and research at the highest international levels of excellence.

Information on this title: www.cambridge.org

First published 2015

20 19 18 17 16 15 14 13 12

Printed in Poland by Opolgraf

A catalogue record for this publication is available from the British Library

ISBN 978-1-84565-385-9

Acknowledgements

© Cambridge University Press 2015
www.cambridge.org

Illustrations by Judy Brown
Cover design and layout by me&him
Authors: Gill Budgell and Kate Ruttle

ISBN 978-1-84565-385-9